More Than Just Candles:

How to **Hygge** Your Mind, Space and Life

EMMA JANSON

CONTENTS

INTRODUCTION

Several months ago, I visited a dear friend of mine. It was a dark and cold Saturday night in the dead of winter, and he invited a few friends, including myself, over for dinner. When I arrived, he greeted me at the door with a big hug and a smile. He was wearing an incredibly soft cream coloured cashmere sweater, thick wool socks, and a pair of his favorite jeans. He walked me into the kitchen where a beautiful spread of cured meats, cheeses and different kinds of olives, fruits and nuts were laid out on gorgeous ornate, vintage serving trays. There were wine glasses set out for each of his guests, and all of his dishes, food and flatware were carefully selected to look beautiful together. Tea candles dotted the shelves and windowsills. He served us a lovely meal with pasta, salad, roasted meats and Italian wine he had chosen specifically for our food. We had a long drawn out meal and chatted about our families, our work, our lives. We shared jokes, laughed and just enjoyed each other's company.

We didn't know it, but we were having a magical hygge evening.

What is Hygge?

Hygge, pronounced (hoo-gah), has been described as being "consciously cozy", or an act of creating a safe and comforting environment. There is no direct English translation for "hygge", but definitions which come close point to terms like cozy or coziness, charm, content, and warmth. The most important thing to understand is that it refers to a feeling - the feeling of being content, and experiencing coziness and warmth. To expand on that definition a little, the word also expands to describing the recognition of value in a simple moment. At its core is an emphasis on the simple things, slowing down, and – this one's important – gratitude.

For the purposes of this book, we'll call making the conscious choice to cultivate this experience in your life *practising* hygge.

Hygge originated in Norway, but was later adopted into the Danish cultural tradition we're more familiar with today. Hygge emerged as a concept to combat the cold, brutal winters in Scandinavia. During certain times of the year in Denmark, it's dark for 17 hours per day. Hygge was the answer to the resulting depression that crept in. It's a wonderfully inspiring concept if you think about it. It shows humans' capacity for adaptability and resilience. We can take the cold, dark, depressing Danish winter and create a concept that has helped develop one of the happiest nations in the world.

A quick google search of hygge will lead you to a lot of advice about decorating and links to places where you can buy fuzzy socks and candles. This is because hygge is partly about setting a cozy and inviting atmosphere, and focusing on the aesthetic of space gets a lot of focus and attention. In this book, you will find information on setting up a hygge aesthetic and making use of a few cozy items, however, you'll also find a lot more. This admittedly North American interpretation of the research on this subject and attempts at incorporating it into my life have led to my understanding of hygge as a state of mind. For this reason, this book shares some insight into how to shift your perspective away from some anti-hygge habits we westerners have ingrained in our modern culture to help you slow down to the pace of hygge.

This book is centered on how to incorporate hygge into your life. As the concept has been embraced outside of the Nordic countries, it has evolved in how it is practiced. Even within Denmark, the term is loosely applied to a variety of situations. Different people have different interpretations of how to practice hygge, and this book offers a broad perspective on how to incorporate it into your life that focuses on mindfulness, and setting up your frame of mind to embrace hygge the way it was meant to be embraced. While the more traditional take on hygge will be noted as we go, the focus in this book is more on how to bring your mind to your hygge practice in any situation, any season, and any time of day.

Bridging the cultural gap

After hearing a bit about hygge, you may notice it sounds a bit familiar. Just because the country you live in hasn't given this concept a proper name, doesn't mean the people around you don't still enjoy it. It's good to name it though, because naming it gives it power and definition. To help you wrap your mind around the concept a bit more, if you're an English speaker, it may help to think of it a bit like nostalgia for today.

Since there is no direct translation, and no identical North American cultural norm to compare it to, I think another way of looking at hygge as being nostalgic for the present. What exactly do I mean by this? Well, consider how we are when we are nostalgic about the past. Think about a time you remember fondly. Are there movies or songs that remind you of those moments? What about smells? Or food, like a particular ice cream store or the roast your grandma used to make? Are there places you go to try and relive old memories and feelings? Relationships you hold onto because of how good they used to be?

It's valuable to have happy and warm memories. If you think about it though, it can make us a little sad, can't it? I had a camp ground I used to go to with my family as a child, and after we stopped going I went back a couple of times as an adult to try and relive those memories. While it was a little comforting to see it again, I actually found it sadder to visit later on. Things had changed, and there was no happiness or warmth in the air. To use an old cliché, it just didn't feel *the same*.

Looking back on the first few years after we stopped going as a family, and remembering visiting old friends, I actually found more comfort in letting go. Moving on and finding new places to make new memories felt better than trying to hold onto the past, even if it was difficult at first.

After laughing with old friends about old times, I find there's really no escaping the twinge of sadness that lingers at the end. Nostalgia for the past, by nature, is haunted. That being said, walking into a shop themed from a previous point in time in your life, or watching an old show from when you were a teenager does give us this feeling of warmth and comfort because it's safe and familiar. With hygge we can feel that same sense of content without sadness creeping in. With a bit of a mind shift, we can feel the same warmth and comfort about our present moments. You probably already do this in some ways without even realizing it. When you prepare your favorite food or go take a walk in a park you really like, you're finding ways to enjoy life right now.

Hygge lets us give little rituals that make us feel warm and happy in the present a name. This book isn't meant to preach at you about living in the moment, but it will offer different perspectives that may help you better incorporate hygge into your life.

Hygge may call to you for lots of reasons

What brought you to read more about hygge? Did you hear about the enchanting Scandinavian spas, or get lured in by the cozy aesthetic? Maybe you read an article about it and were intoxicated by the idea of living the life that ambiance stores keep trying to sell to you. One of perfectly tailored decor, amazing food and great friends. Hygge can help you use those things to enjoy life more, but it's important to remember that hygge is not about material things. This point will be elaborated on later in more detail.

I myself have found hygge through a somewhat tumultuous experience of navigating bouts of anxiety and depression, as well as grappling with the everyday challenges, joys and awes of life in general - all its twists, turns and forks in the road. Whatever has led you here, whether you're looking for a new perspective, struggling through a tough time, or are simply bored and looking for a book to read at the airport, I sincerely hope that reading this book is a positive experience in your life.

Get started

It may seem a bit tough to figure out where to get started. So you can feel like we've made a bit of progress, let's start with your reading habits. Where are you right now? Did you find a quiet space somewhere you like? Your favorite coffee shop? A cozy reading spot you've created in your home? If you have cultivated a nice place for reading, and are using it – congratulations! You're already embracing hygge right now. You might also be reading this somewhere that isn't your favorite – on your commute home on a crowded bus, perhaps. As long as you are using this book to improve an otherwise dull moment, you're on the right track. Some people with hectic jobs and busy home lives love their train commutes and embrace them as a time to read, nap, or just have some peace. Training yourself to look for the positive aspects in any situation is a great way to start practicing hygge.

As I write in this moment, I've created my own quiet hygge writing time. I'm sitting on my comfortable couch in the living room, I've lit a lovely scented candle, and I'm playing music by my current favorite composer – *Message to Bears*. It's a warm summer evening and my window is open; there's a light breeze blowing through my open window, nudging my curtains lazily back and forth. I'm sipping Jasmine tea, and my big white dog is asleep at my feet. I'm working, but I'm taking time to enjoy the moment as much as I can. I'm making an effort to see value in the fact that I have time to spend devoted to something I love to do.

The Commercialization of hygge

As it's been commandeered for commercial use, peoples' understanding of hygge has been vulnerable to distortion. Hygge is a particularly attractive concept to use in lifestyle marketing, and there's nothing wrong with that, but we wanted to talk about it a bit because the explosion of hygge references in the commercial sphere has created potential for people to focus too heavily on material things, and miss out on the real essence of hygge. This book will get into how to leverage décor and cozy sweaters to your hygge advantage, but first, we wanted to talk a bit about how it's being used to sell these things so you can avoid going overboard on trying to buy your way into hygge.

So what is lifestyle marketing?

Lifestyle marketing is a style of advertising that companies use to sell a product or service as something that will enhance your social status. This style of marketing associates its product/service to a desirable mood – like happiness, and/or social status, such as success or youthfulness, to unconsciously make you associate that product/service with that mood/social status. For example, when a beer company runs advertisements featuring groups of young people having fun and camping or partying while consuming their product, that's a form of lifestyle marketing. The goal is to sell you on the potential experiences you could have with the product to sell you on it.

A particularly sneaky method of lifestyle marketing involves brand ambassadors. Brand ambassadors are real people who will post something on social media involving product like a piece of clothing or jewelry, or a service such as a meal at a restaurant or yoga class. They're usually an actual person out in the community who has established themselves as an influential presence. For example, a brand that sells yoga pants may find a yoga instructor who is active on social media and ask them to post a photo of themselves wearing the pants in exchange for money or free products. Basically, lifestyle marketing boils down to advertisements used to make you think your life will be more in line with your ideal vision of it if you buy that product or service.

So what does all of this have to do with hygge?

Hygge itself, as we've discussed, isn't a tangible thing you can buy. It's associated with moods, like a feeling of "content-ness", warmth and peace, and social experiences such as enjoying time with loved ones. Now that we know lifestyle marketing focuses on how an ad makes you *feel*, you can see how the desirable emotions and experience associated with hygge make it a perfect target for lifestyle marketing. Companies can connect it to all kinds of products and services - candles, blankets, cozy clothes, spa getaways, home décor; anything that can be framed as something that could "help" you incorporate hygge into your life could be easily sold with lifestyle marketing. There's nothing inherently wrong with marketing, but take note that if you try to understand hygge through ads disguised as blog posts, you'll miss out on what hygge is really about - connection, love and warmth - nothing that can be bought in a store.

Not just a lifestyle trend

As I mentioned before, if you search hygge online, you'll find a lot of articles using it to sell something, but you'll also find a few referring to hygge "having a moment" or being the "latest lifestyle trend". A trend is the opposite of what hygge is; it's been around for centuries, and just because the internet didn't know about it until recently doesn't mean it's a passing trend or something you can only benefit from while it's in fashion. It was around long before lifestyle bloggers were a thing and will be around long after.

Hygge gained quite a bit of popularity in the last few years, however, these references to trendiness and the frantic doting it has received are not what hygge is all about. This discussion of its popularity creates a sense of urgency and feeling that you're missing out if you don't incorporate it into your life RIGHT NOW. Read: if you don't buy all the hygge things right now. Mentioning it at all when it's connected to a product or service is an effort to sell that product or service, and mentioning its current popularity is to give you that sense of urgency that you have to buy NOW. And guess what? A year or two from now, maybe even already, you'll find articles about why the next lifestyle trend is the "new" hygge and why "everyone" is abandoning hygge in favour of this new thing that, surprise, surprise, requires you to buy a whole lotta' new stuff. And on and on. Wait for the articles titled "why we're over hygge and this new thing is the thing you should obsess over".

Don't worry if you've fallen for it is the past, we get it – it's so tempting to believe those promises. Just, from now on don't buy it. I'm here to remind you what Douglas Adams told us all back in the 1970's. DON'T PANIC. If you try to keep up with it because it's a trend, this will give you the exact opposite affect that you could enjoy if you practice hygge the way it was meant to be practised.

A quick note that this book isn't meant to attack marketing practises or capitalism in general. The only point we're making when we warn the reader against those using hygge to sell products and services is that hygge is a practise connected to an intangible feeling that you'll only be able to get from inside yourself. You can enhance your experience with some material items, but hygge comes from inside you; you can't buy it. It's easier to buy things than reset your perspective, so it's tempting to believe that maybe we can. You can't. We'll repeat it one more time; you can't buy hygge.

This book is ordered in the order of importance regarding incorporating hygge into your life. The first section is on mindfulness, because before you do anything, you need to make sure you're in the right headspace. We're not saying you're more important than your loved ones, but you need to make sure your mentality is in the right place so you can be the best you can be for your loved ones.

The next section, is then of course your loved ones. Hygge really emphasises togetherness as one of its key components, and improving relationships with your loved ones will bring you the most joy and comfort. After that...

HYGGE YOUR MIND

If Hygge is all about spending time with friends and warming up by the fire with cozy blankets, then it seems like all you need to do is make some tea, light some candles and invite your friends over, right? Well, not quite. As with any cultural practice, it takes a certain mindset to really embrace hygge and get a good understanding of what it's all about. Hygge is about incorporating experiences into your life, so it's important to make sure your mindset is in a place that allows this. Before we get into the candles, cashmere sweaters, and spending time with our families, we'll talk about priming our minds to better recognise and appreciate the value in these small everyday moments.

The many different attempts to define it with brevity all have one thing in common, besides the type of atmosphere it describes (warm, cozy and comfortable) it's an *action*. You create it, you make space for it, you are being conscious about it. There's something that you're *doing* – which is making a conscious choice to create a warm and inviting atmosphere, and invite more gratitude into your life in the process. This consciousness is where mindfulness comes in. Mindfulness is important in embracing hygge because practising hygge is centered around focusing on the simple things, and for many people this involves some mental recalibrating.

Mindfulness

So what exactly is mindfulness? A lot of books, articles and blog posts are swirling around about it. It's a favorite concept for internet "listicles" and throw pillow embroidery, but what does it really mean? Simply put, mindfulness is bringing your attention to the present moment. It's focusing on your current thoughts, and what is happening in the present. It sounds simple enough, but it can be so easy to let our minds wander. Whether we're sitting at work and daydreaming about how happy we'll be when our career is ten years more advanced, or in our workout class and thinking about what to make for dinner, we're not being mindful. These may seem like minor things, and we'll all be guilty of it from time to time, but making an effort to be in the present moment and appreciate it for what it is, as it is, is the first step to preparing your perspective for hygge.

It's important to note that mindfulness and hygge don't mean you need to be happy or focused on the positive all the time. That's not a reasonable thing to expect of yourself, because humans naturally experience a spectrum of emotions. The trouble is, we can get bogged down in stress and focusing on too much of the negative, or focusing on things we think will make us happy that, if we pull back the curtain a little, just get in the way of things that will *actually* help us find happiness. These next few sections will give you a few tips on how to be mindful and how mindfulness connects to a successful hygge experience.

Consciously Slow down

An important part of embracing hygge - and this is a big one
– is letting yourself slow down. In the modern world, it's no
secret that many of us put too much pressure on ourselves.
We're too stressed, overworked, and measure our social
status by how busy we are. We can't or won't let ourselves
just be. We have a difficult time enjoying moments and what
is, in my opinion, too much focus on drive, success and being
as productive as possible have led us to always focus on
what's next, and how we can make our lives and ourselves
better. There's nothing inherently wrong with having goals or
planning for the future, but being in a constant state of rush
is bad for our mental health and makes it very difficult for us
to be present in a given moment.

How?

Be honest about how much time you have. If you envision planning
a cozy intimate hygge evening with friends, or spending
Sunday mornings in hygge bliss, but are already panicked
about when you'll find the time then this section is definitely
for you. If you find that you are often failing to accomplish
everything you planned to do in a day, or often feel rushed,
recognise that you only have so many hours in a day, and
rethink how you plan your day. So it's Saturday and you
wanted to visit your mother, do laundry, get groceries and
clean your house. Do you really have time for all of those
things? Try looking at how much time you tend to give
yourself to complete a certain task, double that amount of
time and then plan your day. You'll be surprised by how
much more you will accomplish when you are more honest
with yourself about your time, because you will be able to
focus on and finish a few things, rather than half finish
several things. You'll be able to manage your time because

you'll be more accurate about planning your day.

Stop multi-tasking. When you're doing three different things at once, it feels like you're accomplishing a lot. But try something for me. Pull out a piece of paper and a timer (there will be one on your phone). Time yourself writing the alphabet, and then writing the numbers 1 – 27 in sequence. Didn't take too long, right? Now, time yourself alternating between writing the alphabet and the numbers so: a,1, b,2, c,3 etc.

If you did the exercise, you probably noticed it took longer to switch back and forth, didn't it? The reason is because your brain has to refocus on the new activity every time you switch. So, while it feels like you're doing more, it actually takes you more time, and it feels stressful because it's difficult to focus. Focusing on one task at a time, whether it's laundry, talking to your spouse, making dinner or spending time with friends will help you be better focused in any given moment.

All of this slowing down will ultimately give you a feeling of more control over your life and help you be more in the present moment, not just when you are practising hygge, but when you're doing anything.

Practice being positive

We've all heard the expression – see the glass as half full. It's a tired, overused cliché, and yet it's still widely spoken. Why? Because it's an easy metaphor for how to see the positive in something when you could have just as easily seen the negative. In a world where we're constantly comparing ourselves to each other, being able to see the positive in a situation can help you to fight off those comparative thoughts that leave you feeling inadequate, always wanting more and ultimately unable to appreciate things as they are.

There is a delicate balance between making an effort to be positive and forcing manic energy on every situation and person around you. If you're choosing to focus on the positive, practice letting go of the negative things around you, rather than suppressing negativity. If you buy a container of fresh peaches fruit, only to bring it home and find that they're rotten on the inside, you can focus your mind on being frustrated; go on a mental tirade about how the grocer should be more careful in checking his product, get upset with yourself for not being more diligent, or start getting depressed about the money you wasted. It's easy, and maybe everything you're thinking is justified. But, when you hear those thoughts sinking in, try to find the positive anyway; isn't it lucky you didn't need them for a particular recipe or special occasion? Maybe learning from this instance will make you remember to double check for something similar when the stakes are higher. Or these little annoyances are helping you build a tendency towards positivity for bigger events when you'll really need the resiliency. Whether the "bad thing" was rotten luck or your own fault, learning to live in a world that is at times unfair, and learning to forgive ourselves, are both undoubtedly needed to remain positive and open to warmth, gratitude an appreciation. These little annoyances are actually just positivity practice, and now that you see them that way, you'll find yourself a little hopeful for a minor annoyance to come upon you so you can practice your new skill.

Hygge is about seeing the beautiful in the everyday, enjoying ordinary moments and generally being appreciative of the world around you. The more you practice being positive, the easier it will be to enjoy ordinary moments and ordinary things like your living room, *à la hygge*.

Practice being grateful

Gratitude is a big part of integrating hygge into your life. While we touched on it in the previous section, it still merits its own space. Being grateful for the small things in life, the relationships we have and the things people do for us helps us to get into a head space where we can really welcome the little beautiful things into our lives.

It's easy to promise yourself you'll be more grateful, but can be difficult to consciously practice. To start integrating gratitude into your life, try beginning each morning by writing down (or even thinking about) 5 things that you're grateful for. It could be a family member, hot coffee, warm summer days, your employment, anything. Try to change it up day by day, and challenge yourself to think of different things. If you write them down, look after a week or a month and see how many things you were able to think of.

This can also be a helpful tool for when you're feeling down or having a bad day. When you feel yourself get overwhelmed or stressed and need to take a few minutes, try reminding yourself about something your grateful for to help you gain perspective. If you practice this on more occasions, it will become easier to appreciate the simple pleasures of hygge, and the time you'll spend with loved ones while you practice hygge.

111111111222211

Meditation

There is no better way to incorporate mindfulness into your life than through meditation. Meditation has helped thousands of people refocus their minds. This can be helpful with slowing down, focusing on the positive, and being conscious about our choices, words and actions. Meditating is about focusing your mind on either nothing, or something like your breath. In the practice, when another thought creeps in, you observe it and let it go without judgement. Overall, the practice helps you to stay present and focus on moments in your daily life, which will help you to experience the joy of hygge, since you won't be weighed down by outside thoughts, distractions or worries.

While meditation will certainly help you prime your mind for enjoying the benefits of hygge, it can be a difficult concept for many people, for many different reasons. When we think of meditation, some of us are quick to think of the practice as extreme. For some of us, images of monks in orange robes in a faraway country, or quirky celebrities on T.V come to mind. For others, maybe you tried it a few times and fell asleep, or you found it impossible to sit still so long. Still others, and this may be a harder one to admit, may balk at the idea of being alone with our own thoughts for so long. If this sounds like you, a few ways you can try to introduce meditation into your routine are to start with 3 or 5 minutes at a time, or walking meditation. Meditation isn't essential to hygge or more part of Danish culture than any other, however, it's a great idea for people who have a difficult time being present, which is an important part of really experiencing hygge.

HYGGE YOUR SPACE

Whether you're living in your home town, building a life somewhere new, or live a nomadic existence, you can hygge your space.

Hygge isn't all about the aesthetic, however, setting up your space to make it a bit more cozy will definitely help you achieve that hygge vibe. Whether you are lighting a candle at your desk while you do your homework, or setting your living room up with fall feels, making your space *hyggeligt* will help you feel it. To help you understand the concept, you can think of it a bit like *nesting*. Nesting is a common term associated with pregnant women getting their homes ready for their new baby, but it's often used as a blanket term for getting your home clean, organized and feeling more "home-y". Making your space more hygge friendly is similar to nesting, with an added emphasis on coziness and joy. As long as you arrange your space in a way that you find relaxing, you can build a comforting hygge oasis.

This section is broken into your town, home, cottage and office. Since hygge is a feeling and an aesthetic, each section talks about setting up these spaces as well as changing your perspective about them in tandem, to introduce more hygge into each part of your daily life.

Your town

You can't redecorate your town, so finding ways to practice hygge in your town is more about changing your perspective if you don't already see hygge potential there. It's easy to scroll through online photos tagged #hygge and convince yourself you need to be in a picturesque place to really achieve that perfect hygge lifestyle, but the good news is, this couldn't be further from the truth. Since hygge was born from people making the best of a dreary, cold and dark time of year, hygge is available to you whether you live in a small city apartment or on a sprawling ranch in the prairies.

There is a romantic element to all types of towns.

Home

Hygge focuses on the warmth of familiarity, which even the most beautiful landscape can't compete with compared to home. You could be in the same small village you grew up in your whole life, in a small apartment in a big new city, a dorm room, a cabin in the woods, a town house in the suburbs – it doesn't matter. Your home is your space, the space you spend time with loved ones, and the place you can make into your tranquil solitary getaway. Hygge isn't about living in the perfect place or the most beautiful landscape, it's about valuing your space by taking care of it, by arranging what you have to make it a comforting place to melt into.

Life in far away places is often romanticised in photos, films and all over the internet

Many people live in all kinds of places that seem strange to an outsider. The freezing tundra of the arctic, sleepy small towns, and many more. Why doesn't everyone move to a big city or the Oceanside? Well, aside from the many socio-economic and practical reasons, it's partly because it's home. There's nothing quite like walking down a familiar street in your home town, grabbing lunch in an old favorite spot, spending the afternoon shopping for flowers with your mom, cooking with your dad, or any other activity you did with family or friends growing up.

Colours, themes and artwork

Make it your own, if you like colours, use lots of colours! If you prefer earth tones, black and white style, or only like a pop of colour here and there, then go ahead and theme your room(s) that way. Make your home warm and cozy in a way that you like. The one thing to remember is to decorate based on what will give you that warm feeling of bliss, and not what will make you seem "edgy" or "cool" to other people. When you think of people entering your home, focus on how the space will make the feel welcome or happy, and not how they'll feel about you.

One way to incorporate it into your space at home is through art work, or themes. Some people find a connection to nature peaceful, so if you have a few rooms in your home, you could theme one as the garden room, ocean room, and/or sun room. For example, instead of your home office, you could have a garden room; paint it a pastel green, and keep a small plant in it. You can also keep flower clippings in a vase on your desk. The candles in that room can be scented with rain or floral, and you could incorporate a photo or painting of a flower, a garden or a forest. Instead of a cold, metal desk, you could have a desk made of bamboo. It doesn't have to be too drastic, and you could even just start by painting, decluttering and getting a potted plant. The key is to focus on how the space makes you feel; if it makes you feel happy and cozy, it's hygge. If you tried to make it feel edgy or modern or something that was more to impress the people around you, it probably won't feel very hygge.

Declutter

It may seem counter intuitive, but before you get your cozy blankets and candles and repaint your living space, it's time to donate, sell, and throw away some of your stuff. Maybe just a little, maybe a lot. It all depends on your situation. There are whole books out there dedicated to decluttering your stuff that can provide you with way more detail, but essentially, in order to cultivate a space that makes you feel free, calm and happy, you'll probably need to get rid of some of your stuff.

A lot of us hold on to old things; old things we may refurbish one day, old clothes we may fit into one day, things our future children may want. Take inventory of things you have that you haven't used in a while. Is it possible someone out there may make better use of it than you can? Is it time to accept you'll never be the same size you were in high school and let go of those jeans? Or, promise yourself that you'll buy new jeans if you're ever a size 2 again? Things are just tools, utility items. If a piece of clothing doesn't fit anymore, you don't need it. If it's been three years and you still haven't repainted that wardrobe that sits empty in your living room, and you aren't taking steps to reincorporate your furniture refurbishing hobby into your life (or the idea of doing the work puts you off and has led to this procrastination), sell it.

I'm not saying you should get rid of everything you need and replace it with better things. Nothing will weigh your psyche down more than the debt that would burden you with, and that won't make you feel warm or cozy at all. Additionally, if you are trying to reclaim some comfort through hygge, throwing out sentimental items could just make you feel worse. Don't be hard on yourself, just note that one of the easiest ways to liven up your space is to get rid of things you don't need, and find a new appreciation for your favorite things.

Decorate with cozy in mind

When we decorate, we have lots of different things we might focus on. We might look for a certain *vibe;* like chic or edgy or modern. If you're looking to create a hygge oasis in your space, then our first suggestion is to forget all of those things. Stop thinking about what people will *think* when they walk into your house, and starting thinking about how they'll *feel.* If you want your home to feel cozy, warm, inviting and peaceful, focus on colours, textures and images that make you feel those things. While high fashion décor may seem envied by all, making people jealous of your house ultimately won't make them feel like coming back, it won't make them like you more and it certainly won't help you build an authentic relationship (and ultimately authentic experiences) with them. Focusing on making your space feel comfortable and welcoming, on the other hand, will help you build those meaningful ties that make our hygge moments with friends and family so enjoyable.

Make your own Scandinavian spa:

Have you ever been to a Scandinavian spa? You don't have to go all the way to Europe to find one; the style is replicated all over the world, especially in countries with colder climates. They feature hot and cold pools that you can access outdoors any time of the year, and many also incorporate exfoliating treatments, salt baths and aroma therapy into their repertoire. Scandinavian spas are a part of the hygge tradition; their allure comes from the coziness of the spa contrasted with the cold of winter. The aesthetic in a Scandinavian spa tends to be simple, yet elegant, and embraces natural elements with decorative stones, gentle water fountains, candles and wood.

A great way to incorporate hygge into your space is by making your own spa-like oasis. Start by tidying up and putting away all your toiletries so you can fill your space with some hygge essentials. Wood is big in the spa aesthetic, so you can look for decorative wood crates or bamboo storage baskets to keep your toiletries tucked away, while adding a stylish Nordik twist.

Next, invest in some fluffy towels. For Towels, white is a great choice because it reinforces that clean feeling. A cream colour can work too, if you prefer a warmer touch. Some people like a bit of mix and matching, so choosing a nice red with black and white towels could look good too, depending on what makes you happy. The most important thing about your towels, ultimately, is symmetry. Roll them into cylinders and stack them in neat pyramids or squares on your shelf, with the short, flat edge facing outwards. Stack them all the same, and, if you have chosen a few different colours, organise them so they are spaced evenly.

For wall colours, something muted or neutral will help you achieve that chalet or spa feeling. If you really like colours, you could also try a cool pastel like blue or lilac for a more calming effect. Another thing you can do is incorporate unpainted wood onto one of the walls. Wainscoting or barn doors are a great way to incorporate wood into your space. Just make sure you take proper care of it, because wood can get mouldy easily in humid spaces if it isn't installed properly.

Keep your space simple and clean, but add a few smooth decorative stones along the edge of your tub where there is space, and of course, light lots of candles! A line of tea lights along any edge adds an instant hygge flare. If you're having a bath, add an essential oil like lavender or eucalyptus. Keep a dried version of an aromatic flower like honeysuckle in a decorative jar, and sprinkle some into your bath for added effect. Play some relaxing music. Adjust based on what you like to listen to, but there are hours of spa music available on YouTube, iTunes and many other places.

The last thing to keep in mind is ritual. Keep your spa space clean and ready for you to connect to it with a moment of hygge whenever you need it. Enjoy your Saturdays or add a nice moment to your tough Mondays with a bath and your favorite tea or a glass of wine. Treat your morning shower as your time to find some Zen and prepare for the day. Wind down after your trips to the gym with a mini trip to the spa in your own home. It only takes an extra minute to light candles and play some music, plus, the only thing you really need to have your hygge moment is to be present in appreciating the warmth of the water, the cleansing feeling of the soap, and the peace and quiet. We all carve time out of our day to make sure we're clean, so it's the perfect way to start off your hygge practice.

Trinkets

I can't emphasize enough that hygge is not about consumer goods. With its growing popularity, a lot of advertisements for home décor and soft blankets have been masquerading as blog posts on how to hygge, and it can be easy to focus too much on perfecting your material world. Don't get caught up in this mental trap. There will always be a blanket that looks softer than yours, lounge wear that looks more chic and comfortable, and candles that smell nicer. Advertisements are designed to make their products look better than real life, and your world will never look the same as a perfectly polished and altered photograph, even if you were to buy all the same things in that photo and arrange them in exactly the same way. Curate your space with a few items that make you feel cozy, but don't get caught up in thinking that if you buy the perfect items and make your space perfect, you will then achieve that beautiful hygge peace. You won't. Curating your space is a small part of hygge and much less important than changing your mindset. It takes some effort but it is well worth it. Rise to the challenge!

All that being said, we can't just live in empty space, and there are a few material things we can use to help us hygge our space. To help maintain some perspective on leveraging a few comfort items to augment your hygge experience, we'll borrow from minimalism. This seems counter-intuitive, but minimalists tend to place more value on what they own because they don't own as much as the average Westerner. Instead of owning 25 shirts they sort of like, they'll have 5 they really like, for example. So, as far as the hygge trinkets go, make sure that when you do purchase or save an item that it serves a purpose or brings you joy. And remember - all of the world's beautiful things will never fit inside your home. So instead, just hold onto what fits your space and what you need.

Office

Adding some hygge to your office or workspace will probably be somewhat limited based on where you work. If you work from home or are a student, remember that you can still light a candle and settle into a nice moment, even if you are working. When I work from home, I play nice music, light a candle and wear some of my favorite comfortable clothes. In my office at work, I can still wear headphones for my music and make a cup of herbal tea.

From a mental perspective, to find a bit of bliss while working I refocus on why I'm working. And that is, I am using my talents to make a contribution to the world. I am making an income so I can support myself and my family. And depending on the type of work – I am building something that will be useful to others. Reframing your mind is more of a mindfulness exercise than a hygge one, but as we discussed a bit earlier, it helps you to prime your mind so that you can experience hygge.

Shopping

I don't know about you, but I hate shopping. I *Hate* it. Especially in big box stores or endless malls. I find it so difficult to maintain perspective and focus on what matters. When I am trying to pick up a new candle or sweater, heading to the shopping mall always makes me feel like I need to pick up a new version of everything I own. I start getting convinced I need a whole new wardrobe and to completely redecorate my house. They're size are also, in my opinion, impossible to navigate in a short amount of time. I find them overwhelming, and the least hygge place in the world.

It's tough to avoid shopping though! You can shop online, but with the wealth of availability of items online, you can actually end up having the same experience.

So what do I suggest?

When you can, incorporate hygge into your shopping experience. If you buy less, but buy carefully, this can be easy to do, and the added time, effort and lack of convenience there is around buying extra things can save you from cluttering your home and emptying your bank account with a pile of junk you don't really need.

What do I mean specifically? Head to farmer's markets, find boutique stores that work for you, buy local and MAKE LISTS. I can't emphasize enough how important it is to make lists. If you don't make a list, you're more likely to buy things you don't need in anticipation of not wanting to come back to the store.

I'll illustrate with an example. In the springtime, each year there is a week-long festival that celebrates indigenous culture in my neighbourhood. They have music, food, sunrise prayers and many beautiful displays of indigenous culture. I like to visit each year, and part of my visit is picking up soap for myself. Soap is a necessity, so I have to buy it anyway. I could buy it at the drugstore, but instead I buy it from a vendor who handcrafts the soap with all natural ingredients. The lavender soap is adorned with real, dried lavender, and she packages them in beautifully handmade paper. She also gives the different scents whimsical names, like "moon dance". When I buy soap from her, I get to speak to her directly. Over the years I have met her baby son, learnt about how she got her business going, and in passing she's shared little bits of wisdom with me on her perspective on life. She lives locally, and by buying from her I am supporting a local small business. I know her business ethics and where the materials come from. Each time I visit, I walk around, hear beautiful music and meet different people, all of whom share their culture and many of whom share their stories with me. It takes an hour or two, but I go once a year and then I have plenty of soap. It costs a little more than soap at the drugstore, but I can display it as decoration until I need it rather than spend money (and clutter) on an additional decorative trinket I don't need. I'm also eliminating the less pleasing aesthetic of drug store soap.

I made this into an experience in two major ways. First, the people. Enjoying the company of other people is very hygge. While guides on hygge tend to focus on the warmth and familiarity of friends, I like to expand on that by making that warm connection with the people in my community, or even people in a passing town. At farmer's markets and festivals, the weather is warm, there's music in the air, and vendors tend to be friendly and happy to chat about their business, especially if you catch them in a quieter moment. It's easier to appreciate the value of an object when you get a chance to learn about the vendor's inspiration, how it was made and how much care and thought went into its creation. Hit up a market or small town shops with a friend, a loved one or on your own, and open your mind and heart to the people around you.

This is also a great way to buy gifts. Rather than panic each time a birthday or the holidays come up, keep loved ones in mind when you poke around markets and shops, pick up gifts for them when you find something they like, and save it for the next occasion. If it's a unique piece, they're unlikely to find something similar, even if their birthday or the holidays aren't for a while. Summer is a great time of year for festivals, markets and exploring small towns and there's no reason you can't keep your Christmas shopping in mind over the summer. This way, the stress that can mount over the holidays will be alleviated because you'll have been proactive, and you didn't even have to stress and plan – you were just practicing hygge!

Fire

Most hygge articles, books and videos will focus a lot on using candles. In this book, we take that one step further and advocate for a focus on fire in general. We certainly don't mean that you should become an arsonist as part of your hygge practice. That would not be good! No, rather, we suggest you look for ways to – safely – incorporate fire into creating your ambiance, any time of day!

As an element with the potential for detrimental destruction, why is it that people love fire so much? Well, there are many reasons people are drawn to fire, but it works so well to create a hyggelit ambience because of it's natural ability to produce both warmth and light. Moreover, we like the way it moves – it dances, it sways, and all these things put together give people a calming effect that works so well to create a nice, cozy ambiance.

Below are a few different ways you can incorporate fire into your ambiance:

Candles - The obvious first choice as they are a cornerstone hygge accessory. There is something about them that is just so peaceful. The way their flames flicker is a little primal, and more so, just *real*. They're ambient, and you can get them in all kinds of different scents. They're wonderfully versatile – whether you live in a tiny apartment or have a grandiose mantle, you can work candles into your décor easily. Lastly, you can get them on a variety of different budgets! You can also enjoy them any time of the day or year. While many people think of lighting candles at night time or during the winter, I find there is something beautiful about how a candle lights up a dreary rainy afternoon, and adds a little romance to a summer storm.

Just be careful though - there's no need to light a whole pile of them. One or two will do just fine – not only can lighting several at a time get pricey, it's not great for your respiratory system either. When you're using scented candles, keep your guests or house mates in mind. Not everyone likes the same scents, and some people are sensitive. Just use your best judgement to make the best decision for you and your guests.

Fireplaces – If you're lucky enough to have access to a fireplace, whether it's in your home or once in a while in a rental cottage, we definitely encourage you to use it for your hyggelit evenings. With fireplaces, since they take a bit of extra work, many of us don't use them very often even if we have access. Next time you are planning a nice evening with friends, if you have access to a fireplace I encourage you to take the time to use it. Cut one or two of the appetisers you were going to make in order to make time for it, or something else, rather than trying to squeeze preparing it in as yet another activity you need to do to prepare from your evening. Just remember it's all about balance, not killing yourself trying to make a perfect evening.

Bonfires - Finally, if you're in an area where you can have a bonfire, make use of that luxury as if it were a giant candle. Regardless of the time of year, if people are dressed appropriately, everyone loves a good bonfire. Some people automatically associate them with big gatherings, but they can be hyggelit as well. Have just a few friends over and roast some food over the flames. Break out a guitar and get into some folk music. Centre your fun around a fire and enjoy!

Food

Practitioners of hygge will talk a lot about food. Traditional, tried and true hygge moments involve moments sharing food with loved ones. Gathering together to share a meal involving many different gourmet dishes is definitely one way to hygge with food. Traditionally, hygge food has been decadent. Think heavy, rich desserts and meals and appetisers that are more about flavour than health. There is no counting calories when it comes to hygge food – so lay on the salt, fat and sugar!

If, however, you're a committed healthy eater, you can still enjoy hygge food. Take time to pick up ingredients you don't normally get. Cook some delicious recipes you don't normally have time to put together. Look up a few new recipes online and try them out. Food can still be enjoyable at the hygge level when it's unhealthy.

Hot beverages are also very hygge, as is the Christmas season. While they don't have our North American Thanksgiving in Europe, for those of you who celebrate Thanksgiving, note that it is also very hygge. Whether you bust out complicated coffee drinks, your favorite herbal teas or hot chocolates, there are a variety of hot beverage recipes you can integrate into your hygge experience.

Finally, alcoholic beverages are also a big part of the hygge lifestyle. The original hygge drink is a mulled wine called glogg. It's a warm red wine drink you can prepare in a slow cooker by adding spices to a red wine. The spices include things like cinnamon, lemon, sugar, cloves, and nutmeg, but there are many variations of the recipe. The main reason warm drinks are so important is because the warmth helps to promote that feeling of coziness.

Update your lounge wear

With Netflix's popularity growing, it's easier than ever to find awesome lounge wear. While what everyone finds comfortable will differ, the very hygge lounge wear includes thick socks, soft sweaters and big chunky blankets. You don't have to invest in a bunch of wool if you don't like it though, just stock up on some things that are cozy to you. Even if they don't completely match the Pinterest photos of hygge you see. Wait, isn't Pinterest crowd sourced? Upload a photo of what *you* think is cozy, and then you will match the photos!

MAKING NOT SO HYGGE MOMENTS HYGGE

Hygge doesn't have to be about those perfect moments where everyone found their coziest Christmas sweater and you painstakingly chose the perfect Christmas tea blend to serve in your vintage cups. It's also not about those moments where life works out for the best. I'll illustrate with another example here.

One Christmas my spouse and I were visiting my sister in the town she lived in at the time, which was about a seven-hour drive away. Young, broke and employed full time with very modest amounts of vacation, we weren't able to take extra time off to visit her, and relied on the 4 days we got with the Christmas holiday, boxing day and the adjoining weekend. As a result, we spent Christmas Eve in the car.

Far from ideal circumstances, a normally picturesque white Christmas was green that year. We picked up a friend who was hitching a ride home to a town near where my sister lived, and were off. With seven hours in the car together, we had our own party. We blasted Christmas music and sang along to the carols. We stopped at a truck stop off the highway for tea. My friend and I, the passengers, poured a bit of the good Christmas liquor into our teas (the driver didn't, I promise) (I mean, still not entirely legal but what are you, a cop?) and we sipped our Christmas drinks as we barrelled down a cold, dark highway, signing Christmas songs at the top of our lungs. When we got tired of singing we checked out the other motorists on the road and made up elaborate stories about their lives and where they were going (a favorite pastime of mine anywhere, anytime). I don't think anyone would see spending Christmas eve in the car as ideal, but the three of us reflect on that memory as one of our favorites. There was no big Christmas spread - we at cheeseburgers out of paper bags and our tea got cold halfway through - but we still felt that indescribable warmth and comfort you only feel with your loved ones. That's hygge.

To illustrate with another memory, when my spouse and I moved into our new house, we had a similar experience. On our first night, we had to sleep on an air mattress. All of our kitchenware and most of our belongings were still tucked away in boxes, but we wanted to commemorate our first night in the new house with a special dinner. We dropped by the super market and picked up some food that didn't need to be cooked – cheese and crackers, hummus and pita bread, things like that. We opened a cheap bottle of champagne and toasted our first dinner in our new home with plastic cups, sitting on the floor. It was a beautiful moment and I'll never forget it.

Outside

Since hygge originally came about as a way of essentially ignoring the outdoors when they were unbearable (dark, depressing and cold), a lot of traditional hygge centres around the coziness of the indoors. It might seem counterintuitive to practice hygge outside, or at least focus on practising it in great detail. If you go to its foundational elements though, hygge is the art of mindfulness, appreciation and familiarity. Hygge is enjoying any moment or space that helps us feel safe, warm, or peaceful. Nature has so many places that allow us to feel this way, so if it's available to you, I encourage you to take advantage.

You don't have to go far to feel hygge. It's not about living in a serene landscape far in the mountains, or having an oceanside cottage. There is nature to be savored everywhere. I used to live in a suburban neighbourhood far away from the ocean, mountains, or lush rainforests. If I focused on the negative, I would have only seen the areas with repetitive houses and big box stores. But I looked around, and focused on the river that hugged the Northern end of the suburb. When I looked across the river, I could see rolling hills from the vast, undeveloped landscape in the distance. I found a trail where I could go for walks along the river, and in certain places I would pass by glittering water, forest and sprawling meadows. It wasn't a waterfall in the amazon, but it was still a beautiful place to run, think and enjoy the outdoors.

Hygge by the Ocean:

Maybe you live near an ocean, maybe you visit now and again, or maybe you will only see it once or twice in your life and want to savour it. Regardless, the ocean has been cited as an oasis of bliss and peace in art and literature for centuries, and it is a great place to practice hygge.

There are a few different ways to savour the ocean. Most people like to do this through soaking up the sun and enjoying the beach. That's one way, and we'll talk more about tiki style beaching in the section of this book that discusses summer. But what about the ocean on a cold day? Or an overcast day?

If you've been near the water on a cold or overcast day, you'll know it tends to be much less busy, and a perfect spot for a moment of tranquility. On a cooler, overcast day, head to the ocean in your favorite cozy warm weather wear. Find a quiet spot, on a rock, in the sea grass, somewhere you can see and hear the ocean. Bring a big blanket to wrap around yourself if it's chilly. When you find your space, take time to appreciate the water. Take a few deep breaths to smell the salt in air. Watch the rhythm of the water as the currents move, and the waves tumble. Listen to the waves as they break and tumble onto to the shore. The ocean is a gift of peace, and it's totally free.

This is a great place to read a book, do some sketching or a bit of writing, enjoy a cup of tea, or even just somewhere you can go to quiet your mind. Recognizing the beauty in nature and taking time to appreciate it is great way to practice hygge out in nature.

Rainy Days

Winter is the quintessential hygge season, but I'd say rainy days are a pretty close second as far as seasonal phenomena that need a bit more warmth and love go. Like a cold night, there is something about a rainy day that can feel cozy if you lean into it the right way. Indoors, candles, blankets and warm tea can make a rainy day a peaceful oasis from the busy and sometimes hectic energy of sunny days – it's hazy, it's slow and it's calm.

One way you can hygge outside in the rain is to make sure you have some favorite rain gear. There are so many stylish or fun rain boots and shoes available. Whether you want to wear a trench coat over a black dress with bright pink boots, or practical water proof hiking boots with a neutral windbreaker, get something that makes you feel prepped for the rain. Head outside and find some trails and take a walk. Take a walk through the parks or through the city; whatever is available to you.

While you're enjoying the quiet of a rainy day, round out the hygge-ness of your moment by appreciating its beauty. A sunny sky can be nice of course, but head out on a rainy day and see how lush and green everything is. Listen to the rain drops fall onto nearby ponds and rivers. Appreciate how quiet it is - almost like the stillness of the night visiting the security of the day time.

Lastly, remember that hygge doesn't have to take a ton of preparation time. Getting caught in the rain is a classic romantic moment we see in songs, poetry and on the silver screen. Why? There's just something magical about getting completely soaked, and suddenly left alone as everyone else dives for cover. It represents a type of cleansing you can let ruin your day, or you can embrace. So if you're walking home from the beach and you've still got 20 minutes to go and it starts to pour, embrace the feeling of wet on your skin. Enjoy the moment and remember that many of life's beautiful moments come to us without warning. Practice hygge and embrace them.

Off-season

Hygge was made for the off-season. As we've already mentioned, it was made to combat the dark blues of winter. This makes it a tailor made state of mind to tap into to embrace the off-season.

I'll give you an example with a personal story. I lived in Sydney, Australia for a while. The love of my life came to visit me and see the sights. He was only able to visit me in May, a colder month in Australia. Nowhere near cold like a Danish (or Canadian!) winter, but cold all the same. Like true Canadians, we weren't going to let weather stop us from hitting the sights, and he wanted to see Bondi beach.

On a cold, windy, overcast day, we bundled up in outfits the perfect combination of beachy and warm. We layered so we could hop into the ocean for a few quick minutes. Since the weather was so cold, when we got to the beach, the only people by the water were the lifeguards. The water was surprisingly warm and even though the sky was stormy and grey, the water held an aqua marine colour. The waves were rough, but since we were so used to lake and rivers, we were having a great time enjoying the novelty of their huge splashes, and the tug of the water as it rolled in and out of shore. We didn't stay in the waves for long, but we had one of the world's most famous beaches entirely to ourselves.

When we got too cold, we wrapped ourselves in big plush towels and ducked into a beachside bar and ordered Irish coffees. We warmed up by a heater and watched the ocean churn in the gloomy weather.

It would have been easy to be disappointed by the lack of sunshine, but if you practice hygge you'll find it gets easier to seek out the potential for a great experience in seemingly. Thinking creatively and tapping into your brain's amazing ability to adapt are crucial aspects to bringing hygge into your life on a deeper level, and in moments beyond fluffy quilts and candles. Don't limit yourself to the popular sound bytes associated with hygge, and you'll find you can bring it into your life any time, anywhere.

HYGGE IN ALL SEASONS

Hygge is traditionally connected to winter, but it can be practised in all seasons.

Winter

Peace of the winter aesthetic, blankets, fire places Hibernating: staying in with a good book

You'll notice in this book we've looked for a lot of unconventional, or non-traditional ways of practicing hygge. In this section about winter, however, you'll learn a bit more about the traditional way Danes, and you, can integrate hygge into your life. As previously discussed, hygge was created as a means of combating the winter blues. Their long, dark winters can make people very depressed. They can't really go outside, they don't have enough light, and people tend to socialise less.

The classic hygge aesthetic and the feeling it invokes comes from contrast. There is something satisfying about looking out the window at a windy, snowy evening and being under a cozy blanket in a warmly lit house, wearing your softest sweater with a fire roaring beside you.

The Christmas season

When you think of the holiday season that surrounds Christmas, you'll probably think of twinkling lights, parties, spending time with family and delicious food. If you have experience with other celebrations from this time of year, you'll likely find that many different cultures emphasize the same traits in their winter holidays. There are so many celebrations over the winter solstice because many different cultures have noticed the need for hygge – they just didn't call it that. Cold, dark nights need warmth and light and good food and company are the best ways to capture that need. While the concept of hygge has expanded far beyond its origins, the Christmas season is where it all began.

If you want to align your headspace with hygge in the Christmas season, it's important to focus on a few details. First, a hygge Christmas is *serene*. Forget the craziness of the shopping and the over the top parties. Hygge isn't about a jam packed December schedule or lots of presents under the tree. Instead, it's about enjoying the season for those foundational cultural reasons we all love the season so much. Whether or not your religious, the season is about spending quality time with loved ones. Make sure you take time over the season to see friends and family, and focus on your loved ones as much as you can. Ask questions about their lives. Listen more than you speak. Have extra compassion. Remember that your time is more valuable to them than anything you can bring them.

Another thing you can do is put a hygge twist on your typical traditions. Instead of (or as well as if you like) a Christmas tree, put up a thankful tree. A thankful tree is a tree with ornaments that have things written on them that you're grateful for, rather than ornaments. Or perhaps you can start by adding thanks to the tree. Either way, adding some gratitude into your Christmas traditions will help you and your family to slow down to a more serene hygge Christmas. If you're decorating, keep things peaceful. Avoid flashy lights and go for calming colours and candles instead.

Spring: new beginnings, hope, wonder

There is something I love to do at the beginning of each spring. In my region, we get a lot of snow. The snow can stay for 6 months, sometimes longer, and the cold lasts even longer, with the dark along with it. Like the Danes, people in my region can start to get a little depressed by the whole ordeal, each year.

As soon as the temperatures climb above zero, the big melt begins. Even though there is still snow everywhere, there is a lightness in the air as everyone breathes a sigh of relief and welcomes another spring. When this finally happens, enter the things I like to do.

I find somewhere quiet, usually my backyard, to go during the day and just listen. If I listen closely, I can hear the sounds of water trickling, even though I can't see it, and it isn't raining. It's the sound of hundreds of tiny little streams flowing under the banks of snow as it melts away and prepares the grass and flowers for their lush debut. I love that sound. But I can only hear it if I really pay attention. While I listen, I also like to take a big breath of the crisp air and smell the coming spring. The snow banks have a worn down loo; like they've given up for the year, and there is this general sense that there is a light at the end of the tunnel. The beginning of spring is cold, wet, muddy and colourless, but it's more full of hope and anticipation than any other time of year, and I like to take time to appreciate it.

Regardless of what spring looks like in your region, if you want to keep hygge in your life all year 'round, its important to embrace the spring time with the same care and attention you did when you got your hygge on with soft blankets and warm fires in the winter season. Open your windows and listen to the warmer winds and thunder roll in; light a candle with spring time colours and scents. Spend a rainy afternoon planning out what your garden will look like; whether you'll have a few potted herbs on the windowsill or a whole yard full of vegetables and flowers. If you just have one basil plant, read all about the different recipes you can make, the different ways to prune and take care of your basil and the different breeds you can buy. Slow down, embrace the season and go for a nice walk with your dog or a loved one on the first day it's nice enough outside. How a few friends over and make spring time themed cocktails and snacks with fresh herbs and the early season veggies.

Remember that though winter can be the trickiest season to get through, in our current sometimes hectic and "busy" lives, in the modern world where many of us spend a lot of time indoors unaware of the time of day (forget season) anyway, it's more important than ever to find time to slow down, pay attention to the relationships in our lives and enjoy life. Sure we need to work, contribute, keep a roof over our heads and push ourselves to be challenged, but it's so important to find balance. But you don' t need me to tell you that, you wouldn't be reading this if you didn't already know.

Summer: warmth in the air, lush greenery, relaxed atmosphere

Personally, I find that summer can be stressful. Why? Because it's so short. Ask the average acquaintance or shop owner how they feel about summer in Canada and most people will say they love it. My friends and family feel the same. I love it too, but because I love it and it's so short, I find the expectations for the season and all of its magic can be overwhelming. On a sunny Saturday when I have no plans, a million writing deadlines, a pile of laundry to wash, groceries to buy and a house to clean, I sometimes feel a bit paralysed. I feel guilty that I'm not taking time to enjoy this beautiful and precious weather, and I also feel overwhelmed by the amount of work that needs to get done. On a cold or rainy day, it wouldn't feel so bad, but I feel like I'm wasting gold if I don't enjoy every last second of the summer. On the other hand, I'm not in a position where I can take the whole summer off from work, and mundane tasks like laundry and groceries need to get done eventually. As someone who has neglected those things in favour of "living life" and doing fun things a few times, I can tell you that after a while it's its own kind of stress.

So while there are many ways to find hygge and embrace the summer, I thought it was important to preface with this other, darker side of summer, because I don't think there are any shortages of information out there on how to enjoy long stretches of daylight and warm weather.

Now for the fun part. If summer is already warm and light and exciting, is it really the best time of year for hygge? The answer of course, is yes.

Cozying up under blankets by the fire and lighting a million candles are the last thing we want to do when the temperature climbs, but that doesn't mean we can't still find those feelings of inner cozy – content, slowness, happiness – by leaning into the season of summer.

Having beachy décor around your house is definitely one way to create a serene atmosphere. Photos or paintings of the ocean or shoreline have an unmistakable calming effect on our psyches. There's just something comforting about the water that humans are drawn to. You can also incorporate some light nautical themes into your cushions, throws and statement pieces, like a decorative anchor on the wall. Even just going with a colour palette the same shade as the waves would be a lovely way to embrace the summer vibe and still keep things relaxed.

Another thing to do is really take advantage of the plant life available to us in the summer season. Grow some fresh herbs by the window. Take some fresh flower clippings from the market or your garden and place them in a vase. It seems small but little things like this make a huge difference.

While you may want to ease off on candles this time of year, there are vaporisers and incense and other ways to incorporate a nice summer scent into your home. There are so many different scents out there that capture summer breezes and flowers that you can try. If you're lucky to live out of the city, you could also simply open your windows and let the breeze carry the summer into your home.

Fall: hot cider, pumpkins, plaid and your favorite socks

If winter is the quintessential hygge season, fall is a close second. We love fall for its flavours (pumpkin spice, anyone?), beautiful colours and unbelievable fashion. It can seem easy to gloss over how obviously fun fall can be, but remember this is when the dark and cold starts setting in, and if you don't take care of your mental well-being it can easily zap away your energy and leave you feeling less than content in no time at all. Don't get too caught up in the madness of doing all the fall things. Start slow. Pick up a nice pumpkin (you can take some of the advice from a previous section and make a day of it by heading to a farmer's market or pumpkin patch) to add some nature to your indoor vibe. Light a candle and curl up with a book under a favorite blanket. Take an afternoon to bake some fall themed treats to share with loved ones. Love the season as its happening – if you can, take a hike to enjoy the changing leaves. When you're walking from your car or the bus to the office or the gym, look around and admire the colours. Smell the air as it starts to turn crisp. Buy a nice scarf to keep you cozy in the chilly weather. Curl up with a loved one, an old ghost movie and some popcorn. Find little ways to enjoy the season, but avoid getting caught up in the crazy of trying to do it all.

HYGGE YOUR LIFE (TIME)

Even though we tend to gravitate towards images of idyllic décor when we think of hygge, it`s really more about turning inward and focusing on experiences, relationships and deliberate action. We have gone over what hygge is, we`ve prepared our mind and our space to be open to practicing it, and now it`s time to learn a bit more about how we can adjust our behaviour to welcome hygge into our lives.

In this section of the book we`ll get into ways you can spend your time, both alone and with loved ones (and in some cases, either/or), that are more in line with the hygge mentality. From finding deliberate activities, to reconsidering relationships with friends, family and even strangers, here you can find ways to make your smile and/or look of serenity and content, genuine rather than forced for the benefit of a camera or the people around you (at least mostly).

Make time for hobbies

Hygge is about taking time to be in the moment, be introspective and reflect. Picking up a new hobby or embracing an old one is a great way to enjoy a peaceful moment, either in solitary or with others.

Getting into a hobby, like playing a musical instrument, knitting or making crafts, can help you refocus your mind by giving you something practical to focus on with your hands. If you're one of those people guilty of over-focusing on productivity, the concept of a hobby may not sit well with you. What if you know you'll never be a good enough guitar player to make money in a band? Or what if you know your knitted blankets won't ever sell for a price worth the craftsmanship and time you put into them? It's easy for some of us to put too much emphasis of our productivity. You think that if something won't help you succeed financially, what's the point? This is one of the many places where that shift in focus we keep talking about comes into play. How are you defining success? Is it strictly by monetary value? What if you defined success by the joy you were able to bring others with your gift? If you're playing an instrument, success can be playing at an ability that allowed you to entertain your friends at gatherings. Or your crafting led you to make beautiful gifts for loved ones.

Take it a step in a different direction, what if you had another prong for success? What if your definition of success when playing a musical instrument was playing a song that helped you relax after a long day, or finding a craft that made you feel joy while you made it? An over focus on monetary success can lead us to a place where we don't see value in anything beyond how much money it can bring us, or perhaps how much time we can save.

This can be especially difficult for those of us who are providing for others. People you love depend on you, so of course your focus has to be on providing them as much as possible, right? There are two lines of logic we'd like to challenge there to still convince you to pick up a hobby that will bring you joy. The first is that our loved ones needs us for more than the financial stability we bring them. If people depend on you, you definitely need to prioritise delivering the essentials, however, you'll also need to decide what's enough. Yes, your family needs food, shelter, clothes and a few other things, and maybe even a few luxuries, but they also need your time, and they need you to be mentally healthy. A child needs the necessities and happy, engaging parents more than they need every toy they could ever want and parents who are stressed.

If you are making an effort to build a community around you, picking up a new hobby is the perfect way to meet other people. Because of the internet, it's never been easier to meet like-minded people who want to engage in the same activity as you do. Find meet-up groups in your local area for people who like to knit, read, go for hikes, or any other activity that brings you joy. For those of you who live alone and/or are trying to settle into a new city, this is the perfect way to make some new friends and build some new bonds. If you find that there is no meetup group in your town for the thing you're interested in, you can always try starting one. Worst case scenario, you don't get any responses and move on to the next thing. Best case scenario, you meet a bunch of people who also love the hobby that you do and are grateful that you took the time to set something up for them.

Remember to create

Find something to fill your time that gets your brain or hands working, and gives you something to show at the end of the day. This could also double as your hobby, but doesn't necessarily need to. Things like crafting, colouring (yes, even for grownups!), and journaling are all very hygge. Why? As we age, our schooling and work lives have a way of gradually taking the creativity out of our lives (regardless of how much the modern business world screams for "innovation"). Our creativity is often confined to creative problem solving, but rarely do we get to take colours to paper and just see what happens. No rules, no restrictions, just paint or words or coloured beads or whatever you feel like using as a creative outlet. Finding a way to be creative simply for the sake of it can help our mental wellness the same way yoga and meditation do. It helps you engross your mind in a task that requires active cognitive function (unlike watching T.V. or reading a book), but is low stress (unlike work).

Hygge in the big moments

Traditionally, discussions and practices of hygge revolve around savouring the smaller moments. That being said, sometimes we can lose our way with the "big" moments too. So, for those of you who need a bit of help slowing down for life's big moments, this one's for you.

What are life's big moments? Well, that's really up to you. When I mention them, I think of those moments everyone remembers. Some of them are moments we know are coming; the day you graduate, get married, have a baby. Some of these moments are ones that find us unexpectedly; a first kiss, meeting a new friend, an unexpected and breathtaking view we know we'll probably only see once. Moments we really want to savour.

In modern times, we're often bombarded with a lot of messages. A common one woven into the plotlines of everything from our favorite book, to a peanut butter commercial and the advice your grandfather passes down, is to *enjoy life*. You only live once (#YOLO). Live each day as though it were the last. I think with all the *live, love, laugh* paraphernalia cluttering every other home and quotes around the joy of life on everyone's throw pillows, we're actually hearing it a little too much. What are the consequences of this? Well, two that I can see. First, it's making some of us paranoid that we're not living in the moment enough, and second, it's misdirecting many of us into trying so hard to live in the moment that we miss it entirely.

Where did all these life crusaders come from, anyway? Who are all these people supposedly walking around refusing to believe they should savour the joy in their lives and not realising loving and laughing are good things? And living? I don't think anything makes us all panic quite like being reminded of our mortality, or that we're wasting it. Make your years on this big blue ball count, but don't waste them getting stressed out about wasting them. In the words of a dear childhood friend of mine who I don't call enough, *that's just silly.*

So to conclude this point - to prime your mind as we talked about earlier - to enjoy the big moments, it's probably best to first stop worrying so much about wasting them. This also means (pay close attention, perfectionists) not to worry about making them perfect. They won't be. Think of your favorite wedding, either from real life or a movie. Did it go perfectly, or did it have a few quirky, unexpected mishaps? Did it rain when it wasn't supposed to, did the ring bearer refuse to put on his suit and show up in a super hero costume?

My sister went to a wedding once where the bride took a bad fall and knocked out her two front teeth. The bride took it in stride, and refused to let it ruin her big day. As a result, there are several photos of this bride grinning a semi-toothless smile, and they've got a bit of extra sparkle because she was so happy that even losing her two front teeth didn't bother her. She'd married the love of her life, and so, her reason to smile remained. The big thing is enjoying the reason for the big moment. The little details that we focus on trying to make everything perfect? They don't matter. Someone will forget your rose petal cones in their car. You'll be so nervous you forget to put your veil on. You'll get a speeding ticket on the way to the ceremony. You'll spend your childhood dreaming of a big white wedding and only be able to afford a small ceremony. Whatever happens, around it, as long as you still get married, that big moment in your life will still be there, yours to savour, just don't rob yourself of it. And remember this for the big moments in your life – whatever they are to you.

HYGGE FOR THE TRAVELER

Hygge is centered around comfort, home, familiarity and friends. It seems counter to everything the traveller is seeking in their experience, but as a traveller or a Nomad, you can practice hygge too.

Whether you're a home body looking for comfort on an occasional work trip or vacation, a frequent work traveller or born to backpack, you can hygge on the road just like you can in your living room. Maybe you're skydiving and surfing most days, or maybe you're conducting a lot of business, or maybe you're just on vacation and have a difficult time relaxing outside your home environment. Whatever the reason you are travelling, you are likely outside of your comfort zone. There are a lot of wonderful experiences to be had by pushing the boundaries of your comfort zone, but it's still ok to seek a bit of comfort in your day, even when you're globe-trotting. In fact, knowing when it's time to take a break to recharge will help you seek out more exciting experiences, and enjoy your travels more.

Here are a few suggestions:

First, *know yourself.* If you're a home body and you need a lot of space, you may need to take some hygge time for yourself more that your nomadic, extroverted travel buddy, or the girl you follow on Instagram who's always taking photos of beautiful places every other weekend (who by the way, you should have stopped following by now if she's stressing you out. We talked about this). If you are the extroverted free spirit born to fly, remember we all need a bit of alone time, home and space, regardless of what our Myers-Briggs profile says.

Have comfort clothes. Comfort items don't have to be big, or even impractical. If you're on the road and feel like you need a moment of hygge, pull out an outfit that brings you joy. Maybe it's your favorite pair of shorts and a simple t-shirt. Maybe it's a cozy sweater and your favorite rain boots, or your favorite dress. Many people link hygge clothes to lounge wear, yoga pants or pyjamas, because of hygge's connection to a sense of comfort. However, hygge is a feeling, so whatever brings comfort to you can qualify as your hygge clothes. Whatever it is, have an item that makes you feel happy and comfortable that you can wear when you want to get your hygge on.

Have a hygge routine. Just because you're moving around, or not in your usual space, doesn't mean you can't develop a travel routine. People tend to find comfort in routine, and this is a relatively easy way to find familiarity in an otherwise foreign place. Find a café each morning where you can comfortably read a book or the paper while you have a morning tea or coffee. Go for a walk around your new neighbourhood in the afternoons. Find a local place where you can sit at a bar and have dinner or watch the local sport and chat with other travelers and locals.

Whatever your hygge routine is, just be sure to choose something that suits your personality and interests. Hygge is about enjoying the company of others, and nothing gets you out of your own head better than interacting with other people. Especially if you're travelling alone, try to incorporate speaking with another person into your routine. It doesn't have to be too complicated, it can just be waving at friendly locals on your walk or chatting briefly with the barista at the café. Humans are social (even the introverted ones!) and we find comfort and warmth in interacting with other people.

That catch is that when we're uncomfortable we lose our confidence and our nerve, which can make it difficult to interact with others, so just try to remember that you`ll feel better once you make that connection with others. When you're travelling, the warmth from the interaction could come from a shared sense of comradery through enjoying travel, the sport you're watching, or the coffee you're drinking.

If you find yourself enjoying venturing out into the city to interact with others more than your travel buddy(ies), split up for a bit. You'll want to have the energy and appreciation for your friend or family member when you're sharing experiences together, so if you find it makes sense to split up for a short time to do things that suit your individual interests, that's fine. Friends and family are important for hygge, and can absolutely be incorporated into your travel hygge routine if they are with you, but taking space when you need it is important for balance. Don't feel guilty for taking a bit of you time, just make sure you're present when you return to your travel companion.

SHARING HYGGE WITH YOUR LOVED ONES

Family & friends: build a sense of community

I never gave much thought to the concept of a house warming party until I had my first big move. I always thought of them as a fun excuse to have friends over, or (depending on who was throwing the party) a pretentious excuse to show off your new stuff. I never actually thought of it as a way to "warm" your house, but more of a cute concept.

Flash forward to my partner and I moving into our first house together. I had moved from a childhood home to his house he shared with his brother, with the odd temporary apartment in between. When we got our first house together, it was the first place I had ever really cultivated a *home* as an adult. Everywhere else I had lived had always felt so temporary because it was either student housing or me adapting to choices someone else had made. I was starting a new job at the same time (a coincidence in time I don't recommend, if you can avoid it) and we were changing neighbourhoods. I was so excited, because it was change I had chosen and worked hard for, but my excitement kept me from paying attention to the challenges I would face with that much change. As a result, the first few weeks in the new house were surprisingly difficult. After spending my day in a challenging and foreign environment at work, I came home to another alien space. I couldn't put my finger on it but it just didn't feel like *home*.

I shared my feelings with a couple of trusted friends and family members. The advice I was given was that I needed to decorate. *You'll feel better when you unpack. You'll feel better when you decorate and make it your own.* So, I painted the kitchen a sunny pastel yellow, my bedroom a calming lilac and a third room a Zen green colour. I put away boxes, I lit candles. While I felt a little better, I also felt like I was forcing something. In those first few weeks, it just didn't feel like home. The few inconveniences of the new location and space were highlighted and staring at me, and even though they were far outweighed by positives, they were all I could see at first. I worried I'd made a mistake.

When we were a bit settled, we decided to have a house warming party. We invited friends and family to see our new house, and had a fun night of entertaining them. We made new memories, and shared our space with them. As time went on, we had more events with friends and family big and small. We also created our own memories, just the two of us. I came home to my partner making me dinner a few times. We had a few cozy nights in on the couch together. He laughed watching me do yoga in the living room. We played with the dog after a long day of work. After a couple of months, I would walk into my new home and feel that warm sense of coming home I thought I had lost.

In the end, it wasn't about the space. I preferred the new neighbourhood, and the new house. It was an upgrade. But, nothing can replace the warm sensation of home, because our homes tend to be filled with memories of our loved ones.

So what does all of this have to do with hygge? Well, when you look at some of the loose translations of the word hygge, a sense of togetherness is often mentioned. Modern interpretations of hygge that have been repackaged for the modern Western world focus more on how to hygge in small doses, and how to do it on your own. We are increasingly isolated, and as hygge is toted as a magic remedy for the stress and business of today's world, a more palatable, easy to digest presentation of the concept is easier for people to accept. All this to say, traditional hygge emphasises coziness amongst friends and family.

Not socialising enough can be bad for the soul. People need each other, and they need light and coziness. The key principals behind practicing traditional hygge are warmth, light, good food and drink, and finally – good company. It can, however, be difficult to connect with others, especially in the modern western world. More and more people live alone, in cities away from friends and family, and in general isolation. With bigger, more urban settings there aren't as many spaces to connect with people from your community routinely, so people don't necessarily build a community around them. A few suggestions are to try chatting with your neighbours a bit, and learn the names of local vendors you see on a regular basis.

Choosing relationships carefully

To share authentic moments with others, you need to surround yourself with authentic relationships built on values that support a mindset that embraces hygge. If you build relationships with people to achieve social status, build your ego, or any self-serving or shallow reason, it will be difficult to have authentic hygge moments, or you'll find yourself relying on the material aspects associated with hygge, and looking like you've mastered it without being able to feel it.

Choosing relationships is tricky, especially because we don't get to choose our family. In the next section, we'll discuss tactics you can use to improve the quality of relationships with people around you. This is more straightforward with friends and acquaintances because we have more agency over these people, we can choose to have them in our lives.

Avoid people who drain your energy

When you begin to form new friendships in your life, or are reflecting on old ones, consider why you spend time with a person. Most of the people we befriend start from proximity; they're classmates, colleagues, neighbours or participate in a shared activity like a sport or meet-up group. We don't befriend everyone we come into contact with though, so why do some people end up being friends and not others? Similar to romantic relationships, we form bonds based on things that attract us to that person. Sense of humour, shared interests, shared outlook on life, etc. In some cases, our friendships rejuvenate us. A phone call or visit from a friend like this is therapeutic. In other cases though, we may find ourselves in friendships with people who drain us. After spending time with these friends, we may feel more anxiety, depression, general uneasiness or other negative emotions. Everyone has an off day, but if you have friends who are draining, it's important to re-evaluate why you invest time in that person, and ask yourself whether the relationship is really a healthy one to continue pursuing.

Friends we make in post-secondary education and at work can lead to tricky, unhealthy dynamics. When we're in these settings, we are driven to form relationships with our peers in the name of "networking". We're taught that it's better for our careers to form bonds with the people around us to help us advance in the professional world.

I'd like to be careful here because I'm not suggesting you shouldn't make friends at school or work. To the contrary, I think it's important to have meaningful friendships within all the communities you take part in. But when choosing the people you invest extra time in, the people who become more than colleagues and classmates and become close friends, it's important to reflect on why you're investing more time in specific people. Without even realising it, we may end up choosing people who seem to be propelling towards leadership, or who have other connections we think could benefit us. Depending on your field, an incredible amount of pressure is placed on people to form these bonds, so I don't want to pass judgement or make anyone feel badly for engaging in this behaviour. Just be honest with yourself. Do you have friends you invest time in because of superficial benefits they either do or could potentially bring to you? Do you find spending time with them draining? To reverse the situation, are there people who, if you think about it critically, spend time with you to benefit from something superficial you have to offer? Perhaps you have a friend you make an effort to spend time with, who never seems to accommodate you into their schedule. It can be hard to be honest with ourselves about the dynamics of our relationships, but having authentic hygge moments can only really be shared with people you are in authentic relationships with.

There are other types of friendships that are draining for different reasons. Perhaps you have a friend who is perpetually negative, or puts you down. Maybe you have friends who engage in behaviour you are trying to grow out of. Whatever the case may be, you don't have to start writing out good bye letters and text messages to all of these people to formally announce that you are no longer spending time with them. What I would suggest instead is just refocus your energy and let those relationships end naturally. If a person asks for an explanation regarding why they never seem to see you anymore, be honest with them, but avoid being negative or judgemental.

Improve the quality of your interactions with family and friends

Once you start re-evaluating which relationships you'd prefer to stop spending time on, you'll start to get a clearer view of who the people in your life you really value are. In this section, we get into how you can apply the principles of hygge to your relationships with the people you really care about.

Enjoy the small moments with the people you love

☐ Life is happening now: living in the moment and being present with friends and family

The single most valuable piece of wisdom that has come from every corner of the world in some shape or form, and is repeated again and again in literature and folklore throughout history, is that our loved ones are the single most valuable thing we have in this world. Our family, our friends, and our partners. They are what give our lives meaning, they bring us love and joy and add a crucial element to our lives that money just cannot buy. In a world with ever increasing demands on our performance in the professional world, in being more *productive* and delivering ever increasing efficiency and quality in whatever line of work we do, it can be so difficult to give ourselves permission to spend leisure time doing anything, and this includes spending time with our loved ones. The energy we spend on other aspects of life can also lead us to withdraw into seclusion on the few precious moments we do have to ourselves, rather than make the effort to spend time with the people we care about. With practising hygge, however, we can savour our moments with our loved ones better.

It's worth exploring why we don't always do this. A common temptation is to value money above all else, and another is to value work as a means to provide for your family, and being unable to decide when it's time to stop prioritising our work for the day. Our culture in the western world can make this difficult. We're taught from when we are small to value school and cultivate a good work ethic. This is a good thing, but it's important to know when to stop working. A common trope we hear is that no man, on his death bed wishes he had worked more. And yet, we find ourselves valuing our bosses' needs over those of our loved ones. Even if we don't think we do, a look at our actions can often be a lot more revealing than our intentions.

A common mistake we tend to be guilty of is treating our loved ones with less kindness than we do strangers. This is a defect of our humanity, and it's easily explained. The very safety and security we develop with our closest family and friends that gives our relationships so much meaning leads us to take their love for granted and forget the value of our relationships with them. We trust that they'll always forgive us, and they'll always love us, so over time we invest less time in them, and are more careful to treat acquaintances or people we are building relationships with more delicacy and care. Even though it's a tendency of human nature, it's important to recognise that we do this so we can make a conscious effort to show our loved ones we value them. We don't have to be victims of our nature, and have the capacity to change our habits once we recognise harmful patterns.

Think about the people closest to you; your spouse, your parents, siblings, friends, maybe right now your family are far away and you only have one friend you lean on. Whoever you are thinking of, I challenge you to do something for them today or the next time you see them that shows them you value them. You may already do this, so try to think of something extra you can do. Maybe you can give them a call on their lunch break to ask how their day is going. Make their favorite meal for them. Join them in an activity they like to do, like a hobby or a workout class. When you engage them in conversation, see if you can ask more pointed questions about how work went or how their kids are doing. Make an effort to remember small details to show them you listen when they speak, and that you care about the little details of their day.

You don't need to buy people gifts or take them on expensive outings to show them you care. While that may be a nice thing to do on special occasions, what our loved ones need from you is *you*. They need you to show them you care. Believe it or not, they need you to listen to those silly stories about that crazy thing their co-worker said in a meeting, or their mom's online craft business. If you put yourself in their head for a second, when they were at work, away from their family and possibly even having a tough day (that won't always be true, but sometimes it will), something a little silly or shocking or exasperating happened. Maybe it frustrated them. In that moment though, they thought of you. They thought about how funny you would find the comment their co-worker made, or they thought about telling you about this stressful moment, and thinking about telling you that story brought them comfort. Remember how valuable you are to your loved ones, and make an effort to show them you care.

This book isn't about relationships, so what does all this have to do with hygge? Well, as we mentioned before, you can't have authentic moments with people when your relationships are inauthentic. So if you try to have a hygge moment with your spouse by buying a nice candle, a cozy blanket and some nice cheeses and wine, but for the last several months you haven't been connecting properly, all you'll have is an unsatisfactory moment with your partner that was supposed to feel comforting but didn't. And, all you'll get out of it is disappointment and maybe a good Instagram photo you can use to keep lying to the world about how happy you are.

I definitely don't advise you to approach your friends and family and announce that you've decided to be more mindful and hygge, hand out wool knit sweaters and lecture everyone about living in the moment. If you find peace and increased happiness through practicing hygge, it will be tempting to try and "convert" your loved ones. I know it comes from a good place. You're so happy and you just want them to feel the same happiness you feel, right? Well, I caution you against the "preachy" method. I promise you that you'll lose more friends than you'll convert if you try to be too persuasive.

Instead, work on improving your relationships and strengthening bonds with your loved ones. Invite them over for a hygge wine and cheese, but don't tell them you're hygge-ing (unless of course they're into it too!). Use all the pretty dishes and candles you want, but focus on having a nice time rather than convincing them they need to hop on the bandwagon. Eventually, people will notice a change in your behaviour and they'll ask you about it. You can share your changed perspective, but do it gently. If people are interested, they'll come to you for more information.

I really want to emphasize the point that you shouldn't have expectations about the reactions of your loved ones when you try to hygge with them. It's possible they may not be in the right place in their lives to broaden their perspective about finding happiness in everyday moments. While I believe anyone can do this at any time, it's not something we can or should try to impose on others. We can share our perspectives on things when the time is right, but don't expect your friends to notice your new views on lie right away, or fully appreciate your actions right away. They may be going through a difficult time, and may not be in a headspace to see it right away. Be patient, and remember they're human just like you, and just like you used to, they're allowed to have times in their lives where mindfulness isn't at the top of their mind.

Be forgiving

I used to wait tables at a local restaurant. On a quiet afternoon, I was serving lunch on one occasion to an overwhelmed mother with two young children. She ordered a glass of apple juice for one of her children. I placed the empty cup on the tray and filled it with juice, without realising the cup was cracked. When I lifted it off the tray and onto the table, juice begin to spill everywhere, adding even more chaos into her afternoon. I apologised profusely and braced myself for her to berate me, but instead she smiled, picked up a napkin and began helping me clean it up, "it's ok, you didn't know", she said.

It was a small act of forgiveness, but it meant everything to me at the time. She turned what could have been an incredibly unpleasant experience for me into a wonderful lesson I still remember years later. In every situation, you have a choice. You can demand exactly what you think you're entitled to all the time, choose to hear offense whether it was clearly intended, and hang on to slights against you, or, you can let go. You can have empathy for the other person, whether they're a stranger, co-worker or family member, and you can choose not to prolong an unpleasant experience.

This is, of course, much more difficult to do in some situations than others. There are bigger, moral offences that are more difficult to forgive. We won't get into the big existential questions, but when a colleague makes a mistake, or loved one forgets to finish a chore, learning to forgive the little things will help you have more pleasant interactions with the people around you. If you show empathy for the people around you, they'll show it in return, and before you know it, amongst your family friends and larger community, you'll be helping to build a culture of respect, forgiveness and peace –

and with peace and harmony, comes hygge.

No controversy in hygge moments

While it's admittedly entertaining to watch while your grizzled, conservative uncle antagonises your tattooed, vegan sister at Thanksgiving, hygge gatherings are no place for controversial debates. True Danish tradition requires you to leave talk of politics, religion, child rearing and any other hot topics off to the side for another day. As a cozy concept, hygge is meant to be warm, welcoming and *safe*. It's supposed to encompass the type of rare moment where your uncle and sister agree to disagree, for the sake of peace. There's a time and a place for lively debate, and I'm not here to say it's bad. Indeed, some people have criticised the Danes for their lack of willingness to discuss the hot topics. But, my westerners, we have a habit of pushing ourselves all day. At work and school we prove our cleverness and wit with our opinions about the world around us as much as we gain any social value in discussing these things. If you're looking to slow down, making time to enjoy the company of those around you in a controversy free zone may be exactly what you needed. For friends and family members who you tend to butt heads with, making an effort to spend time this way could actually help you foster more empathy for them, and have more productive conversations when it is time to debate.

HYGGE ON YOUR OWN

While hygge is traditionally associated with being in the presence of family, there can be many reasons why you'd also want to hygge on your own. Introverts need a lot of quiet time, and family and friends aren't always available when we need some time to slow down. Taking time to just be in the moment on your own can be hygge as well. Grab your favorite book and a cozy outfit, and relax.

Next time you have a free day, or even just a quiet evening on your own, consider making it a hygge evening. Start by setting the scene; make sure that your space is clean, tidy and clutter free. Ensure that you have some cozy blankets and pillows and a nice place to cozy up with a good book or, if you're not a reader, a movie you love. The next thing to do is make sure you have some awesome lounge wear. Think comfort chic – your favorite pajamas or comfortable clothes that are still a little cute or stylish. Why the need for a pop of style? You'll be surprised how nice it feels to be well put together but still comfortable – even if you're on your own. Just remember to go for the cozy – put away the scratchy sweater that looks cute and comfortable but gives you low key hives, bust out those matching flannel pajamas or your favorite lulu lemon leggings.

Next snacks! Whatever your favorite snacks are, make sure you stock up. Or, save up your appetite and a few pennies for your favorite take out place that no one in your family ever wants to order when you order with others. If you're in a place where you're trying to be healthy, no problem! Look up a few healthy recipes with some of your favorite ingredients and relish in how nice it feels to fill your

Emma Janson

body with healthy vitamins and nutrients.

Dig up a hobby you haven't done in a while. When I'm not busy, I like to knit. You may enjoy crocheting or other crafts, or maybe you play an instrument. Regardless, pick up a hobby that you like to do because you enjoy it, not because you're practising for a major event, you make money at it or any other reason. Do something just because you like to create.

Finally – candles! we can't overstate how important candles are to a wonderful hygge night in. You don't need to be having a get together with family or a romantic evening with a partner to enjoy candles. They set a tone that will really pull your day together.

86

Coziness in different times of the day

Even though it was created to bring warmth to dark nights, all different times of the day can have the cosiness of hyggelit. Here are a few tips on how to seek out the cozy any time of day:

Morning – No need for me to go on too long about how peaceful sunrises are. They're spectacular in size and utterly beautiful. If you're up for one, take it in and think about why it's so peaceful. Have a coffee or tea and take in the stillness and the quiet. Mornings can feel rushed, but if you make enough time for them, they can be the most peaceful part of the day.

Afternoon – the afternoon probably seems like the least hyggelit time of the day. But stillness can be found everywhere. Take time out of whatever busy hectic activity you do during the afternoon and shut out the business of the world. Take a walk, take your lunch break – if you enjoy it properly, the afternoons can harbour an oasis that breaks up your day that you look forward to each day.

Evening – Evenings can also be a busy time of day – we're rushing ourselves or our children around to different activities, commuting from work, and trying to find some time to make dinner in there as well. You can find some fun quiet time in the evening if you carve it out though. Like watching the sun rise, watching it set is just as peaceful. Watch it sink on yet another day that you conquered. Enjoy the solitude of your commute and take time to listen to some music or reflect on your day. Grab a nice hot chocolate while you wait at your child's activity.

Night – nighttime is, of course, the birthplace of hygge.

It's when life gets still again, the stars come out and your candles really shine. Enjoy the stillness of the night, and look out for a moonrise if you can see one. I once had the opportunity to watch the moon rise over the Pacific Ocean, and it's quite possibly once of the most majestic things I've ever seen.

Hygge doesn't have to be a big event, but the more you take time to seek out life's simple pleasures and little moments of serenity, the easier it will be to incorporate it into your life.

Love the simple things

Before we talk about material elements that can help enhance our hygge experience, we really want to emphasize that hygge isn't about *things*. It's important not to place too much emphasis on how material goods enhance your hygge experience, because you may lose sight of the more important elements of hygge, which is appreciating time with family. As hygge gained mainstream popularity in the western world, the concept has been hijacked by the retail industry to sell knick-knacks. You don't need the softest cashmere or the most whimsical mountainside winter cabin to experience hygge. As long as you take the time to make your space cozy with what you've got, and to really appreciate the company of your loved ones, you're experiencing hygge.

We've talked about loving the simple things here and there in this book, but just wanted to make sure the point came through clearly. We pick up little embellished tea pots, spend time cooking delicious meals and arranging our houses in ways that we want them, and hygge is about really enjoying things like this. It's also about making the best of wherever you are and whatever you're doing. You can always find a bit of joy, just train yourself to look for it!

Manage your tech - embrace the benefits of unplugging

Whatever your reasoning, you've landed on these pages because you want to practice hygge, which means enjoying the present moment more, and in today's world, this means...I hate the word "unplugging", it makes me feel like one of those strict eighth grade teachers who wears dorky sweaters...so let's say it means some power down time. That works because with hygge we're powering down our brains a bit too, aren't we? Alright it's settled we'll go with power down.

Buckle up, for this section it's long and it has some harsh truths. But, if you really want to be able to achieve the true feeling of content that practising hygge can bring you, learning how to back away from the phones, lap tops, social media and even the T.V. is critical.

Social media

Have you seen any of the blog articles about hygge? Many of them feature a cozy blanket and a cup of coffee. We writers are particularly guilty of sharing cozy photos of coffees and keyboards on a pretty (usually wooden) desk on social media ourselves. Look up #hygge on Instagram or twitter. I'll wait. What do you see? Photo after photo romanticising all the things I just spent a lot of time telling you how to incorporate into real life.

So what's my point? Well, for you social media junkies, you may be tempted to share your hygge moments with a perfectly taken, filtered and captioned photo. But before you do, stop and think about how that loop works for a minute.

You're on Instagram or twitter and see a #hygge photo. Maybe it's of an intimate candlelit gathering, or someone cozying up by the fire reading a book in their cashmere sweater. How does it make you feel? If it's your mom or your best friend maybe you just feel happy for the person, but often times they make us feel envious, or even panicked, like we're missing out on something. These photos are making you wish *you* were enjoying a book beside a cozy fire. So what do you do? You create your own hygge moment and you take painstaking care to photograph it perfectly, as if you need to report back to the internet to validate your experience.

But wait, when you do get to those moments, if you're obsessing over a photo, are you really enjoying your scenery and your atmosphere, or are you preoccupied by making it *look* like you are?

And guess what? That person whose photo made you envious, was doing the same thing. Especially if they're a professional blogger, Instagram model or celebrity. They may even have someone doing it for them. Do you know how many takes those photos need sometimes, to look as perfect as they do? How many adjustments are made to get the colour and contrast just right? My point is, in the situation I just described, one that many an Instagram fan has been in, no one was really having an actual hygge moment. Getting too preoccupied in making it look like the perfect moment stole it away.

So what's my point? I'm not saying you need to let go of social media forever. And for those of you who are pros, some of this is work to you. What I am saying is this: Sometimes, you have to make a choice. For example, if you don't have a lot of time, you sometimes have to choose between enjoying the moment and capturing the moment. If you want more hygge in your life, choose enjoying the moment. Every time.

I'll give you an example. I'm a canuk, and a big hockey fan. My hometown's team made it into the playoffs recently, and it was your typical underdog story. No one thought they would make it as far as they did, but they just kept surprising everyone. So a few friends and I managed to get tickets to one of the games. Our team was losing, but they kept tying up the score when no one expected them to. They went into double overtime, and then, as we all watched breathlessly, we scored! We won the game and went on to win the series.

So back to hygge. When that goal was scored the whole crowd went absolutely wild. The thrill we all felt was intoxicating. We were screaming, cheering, and giving each other high fives. The moment was shared with friends and strangers alike. Now I do remember reaching for my phone in my back pocket, thinking about how cool it would be to get a video of the crowd. I opened my phone, and realised the app wasn't working. Grabbing it in general took me out of the moment, but when I saw that I had to put in passwords and mess around with keys, I had to make a choice. I had to decide whether I wanted a video of that moment, or whether I wanted to keep living it – because the crowd only cheered for a minute, and I didn't have a lot of time. I put the phone back in my pocket and just lived it. Everyone who would have seen my video would have seen a million just like it, as well as a much better shot on the highlight reel. The only thing I would have accomplished would have been elevating my social status a bit by being there, and perhaps making a few of my friends jealous for missing it. We like to joke about making people jealous, but is that really what you want? Would disengaging from connecting with all those people who were physically there, and the joy we were all sharing, have been worth making my friends feel bad, and maybe making myself seem a bit cooler? My personal answer to that is no. I don't want to make my friends feel bad, and I don't want to take myself out of a fun moment in time just to make myself look a bit cooler. I've chosen friends that love me for who I am, and I've chosen to live a life that's in the present.

So now you decide. If you'll end up missing your child blowing out their birthday candles because you're trying to take the perfect photo, is it worth it? Would you rather watch it through your camera lens, or would you rather just be there? Not worry about angles or lighting or catching her smile, but just be there and experience it. We feel a lot of pressure to make our lives look great, even if it's just to keep our own memories, and to capture every moment. Let hygge let you give yourself permission to be in a moment rather than capture it.

I'm not saying you have to stop taking photos completely. Photos are nice to have to remember and relive special moments. What I am arguing for is to take them less, and to re-evaluate *when* you take them. If the act of taking the photo or video will contaminate the experience, how necessary is it? Maybe you only need to take them when you're on a nice long walk, or at a party that will last hours, and there is time to both capture and savour. Find a recipe that works for you. All I'm trying to say is, if you want to live the hygge lifestyle, choose to savour a moment over capturing it. Ask a friend to take a photo of your kid blowing out their candles, just remember not to miss things that matter. We're not here forever, and neither are our loved ones, and I don't think you'll find much comfort going through your perfectly captured moments later in life if it meant you missed them.

All the other tech

Some of us aren't social media junkies, but still struggle with the technological invasion. What about T.V, scrolling through phones, or clicking away at your laptop? No one is off the hook. Are you a business executive who doesn't even know what Instagram is, but you keep a religiously strict eye on the news? I'm talking to you. Do you run a mommy blog? I'm talking to you too.

Think about when you're teched up and powered on for a minute. What are your go-tos? Are you always listening to music, on your laptop, scrolling through your phone? Emailing on a blackberry? Video games? Many of us are at a point where we're actually just full blown wired. I might be at work in front of a computer also intermittently looking at a phone screen. Sometimes at home, I'm watching TV while I'm on my laptop. My phone isn't ever too far away either. Sound familiar? It's crazy what we're doing, isn't it? How are you supposed to turn your mind off when the T.V is telling jokes, the phone is blowing up with notifications and there's something on your laptop you're trying to read? More importantly, If I'm working on my laptop and the TV is on – when my partner comes home and starts telling me about his day, I'm not able to give him my full attention, even if I try to focus. When I'm playing with my electronics and not focused on him, I'm not really communicating that I'm open to engaging with him anyway, am I? He might walk right past me or pull out his laptop and start doing work of his own. This can happen if you have children too. If you're not making an effort to put your tech away, they'll take the signal and power on themselves, probably with double the screens you've got going.

So what do you do? Well, we're all busy, so you have to

make time and be honest about your priorities. Carve out time in the day when you and/or your loved ones can power down. If you live on your own, try exercising outside. Alternatively, just go for a walk through your neighbourhood if you can. Walk to get your groceries. Cook a meal and just listen to music, or open a window and listen to the birds chirping, the wind blowing, or the rain pouring. If you have friends and family around some days or most days, spend time with them. Play games, cook or go outside together. If you have a spouse, partner or anything related, power down when you're in bed. I'm confident you can find something fun to do that doesn't involve the TV or your phones.

A smack upside the head for workaholics, perfectionists and self-proclaimed type A's.

I'm willing to bet a disproportionate amount of you fall under this category. Have you ever sort of half apologised for being "type A" when you were being too militant about something to friends and coworkers? What about lamented about how you're a workaholic or how your career is held in the highest esteem above all else? Have you done any of the aforementioned and then blatantly made no effort to change your behaviour? Did you do any of these things today? Last week?

Workaholics of the world, take a mind journey with me for a second. Generously, you have 100 years to live. You spent the first part of your life going to school, working hard to get good grades so you could pursue post-secondary studies or apprenticeships. You kept working, and kept working hard. Maybe you've achieved some success. Maybe you're only just beginning your working life and hoping for success, or maybe you've reached that point you worked so hard to get to. You have a big office, you have influence, power and money.

But, you're still here, reading this book about chilling the fuck out. Why?

There's nothing, absolutely nothing, wrong with working hard. Indeed, to reach some personal goals, pursue a career in art for example, long hours of unpaid or poorly paid work supplemented with work you don't want to do, is necessary. Finishing school can be tough go of it too. And we don't ever want to think a romantic partner or family could stop us from achieving every dream we've ever had. And that's all fine.

Let's just revisit our dreams for a moment. Working hard is held in high regard in capitalist societies. Want to know why? Because the harder everyone works, the more money the big boss makes. The more money you make, the more you can spend on the economy. The more extra hours you squeeze in unpaid, the more efficient you become, the more money the people above you get. The more hours you work making money as an entrepreneur, the more you're contributing to the growth of the economy. In a society with this type of economy, of course you need to feel pride in working long, hard hours and maximising your productivity. Of course they want you to feel ashamed when you clock out at the exact time you're supposed to every night. They want you to make them more money.

Some of us have aspirations that are noble and take hard work, like the artist, like the doctor who lives to heal patients, or the researcher who dreams of curing cancer. It's fine to work towards goals, but it's important to remember why you have them, and what your priorities in are.

If you always prioritise work over all else, what exactly is it you're prioritising? Money? Power? Influence? Social Status?

Let's start with money. Countless people before me have noted that it can't buy happiness. And more have said that this is only half true. It's true that you need enough money to fulfill your basic needs; food, shelter, a bit of entertainment. But after that, we reach a bit of a plateau. When we keep chasing money after we have enough to live and pay our bills and go on a few vacations, what is it we're after? And could spending money more wisely help to mitigate the need to work more? I think we're sold on the idea of grand luxury when we get obsessed with money. Maybe you dream of early retirement, luxury travel and buying expensive things. But here's the thing. If you're working so hard that you're never enjoying life, you're robbing yourself of the very things you seek. What is it that money can buy that will make you happier than spending time with loved ones? Than having a child you're forcing yourself not to want in the name of professional pursuit? It's fine to work hard, but remember to look at what you're sacrificing versus what you're gaining, or if you're socially conscious, what you're contributing to the world.

Taking care of yourself: exercising and eating well

It's hard not to be familiar with the health craze. At a time when big diseases are on the rise, and obesity in the west is a growing problem, there are all kinds of different methods coming out to try and help people lose weight. While well-intentioned, in the western world we tend to edge along the extremes. We practice denial of everything for a while and then we over-indulge and binge.

While the latest diets centered around regular juice cleanses or cutting carbs make loud noise, you may have also hear some health gurus talk about lifestyle changes. Diets and arduous, extreme exercise routines don't work to make us healthy because they're not sustainable

You'll notice that good food and drink (mulled wine in traditional hygge practice) are a big part of the traditional way to practice hygge. It's important to note that even though indulging in good food is a part of the hygge mantra, over-indulging is not. Regular hygge practitioners don't practice harsh diet restrictions. Instead, they do things in moderation. Don't cut out dessert all together, but when you do have dessert have a smaller amount. Don't cut out French fries altogether, but don't eat them every day.

Exercise is the same. Can you think of a time in your life (maybe a recent January?) when you committed to a new workout regime that was burdensome? Maybe you got a personal trainer and did a gym routine 3-4 times per week that you hated, or joined a class you didn't really like. Having something you hate this much built into your daily routine is both unsustainable and un-hygge. If you want to incorporate hygge into your day, make sure you exercise, but do it in a way that's fun for you. Play a sport you like. Go for lunchtime walks. Do yoga, even if the caloric burn isn't as great as CrossFit. Give yourself a break and find a routine that's fun for you, and you'll find that you'll end up getting the same benefit from it, because you'll stick to it long term and won't skip classes as much. The hygge element to this is finding ways to enjoy your physical fit time, but you'll like the added benefits as well.

Related concepts: lagom and minimalism

You may have noticed that hygge aligned with other perspectives or schools of thought you have heard of before. We're not really here to advocate for strictly following a life of hygge and only hygge, and wants to use this section to share other perspectives that you may also be interested in looking into further.

Lagom

Lagom is similar to hygge, but with more of a focus of balance rather than indulgence. It is a Swedish term that word directly translates to "just the right amount". The concept forms the basis of Swedish psyche and is a cultural phrase referring to the idea that there is a perfect amount of everything. It refers to a favouring of equality in society, and a rejection of extreme consumerism and decadence. If you are familiar with the children's story "Goldie Locks and the Three Bears", Lagom has a similar foundational philosophy – there is a just right amount for everything.

Personally, I've been practising a bit of Lagom every year after Christmas without even realising it. After the rush of the Christmas season, the over indulgence of food and drinks and parties, I like to take down all of the sparkly decorations, do some deep cleaning and have a bit of a "reboot". Like many people, I get more serious about my exercise regime, and I return to healthier eating – more vegetables, less sugar and fat. What I don't do that many people do, is get hyper restrictive. I don't over commit to an unrealistic exercise schedule or fitness goals, and I don't make definitive or grandiose restrictions on what I can eat. I'll still have takeout or desert once in a while, and I don't hit the gym every single day. I just go back to being strict about my routine, and not giving up entirely on my gym schedule or healthy eating like we tend to during the holiday season. If you work towards lagom, you can break out of the cycle of over indulgence and restriction. That's not to say that once in a while you won't still really buckle down and focus on work (like during exam season or when you have a big deadline at work) or that you won't have times of greater indulgence, like the holidays. It's fine to have some ups and downs in your routine because mixing it up keeps things exciting. All we're trying to say is, when possible, try to go for that just right feeling, rather than jumping into an extreme version of everything.

If you find you are the type to over commit, over plan, and try to do too much, this could be the balancing state of mind you need to re-center yourself. Not having enough is a basic need we all want to avoid, but we don't talk about having too much as much. Too much of anything, even good things like relaxation, parties, a delicious food, can make us unproductive, overwhelmed and sick. If you try to incorporate that just right mentality into your life, you may also find that you accomplish more. Look at fitness goals as an example. In the New Year, many of us like to take on new fitness routines. A new year signifies a fresh start, and we're all looking for a bit of wellness after the craziness of the holiday season. Many people promise themselves they'll work out 6 or even 7 days a week, take on a gruelling and difficult routine. They sign onto a year long contract with their local gym, honour the commitment they made for a week or two, and then eventually they give up entirely. When people don't meet the goals they set for themselves, they get discouraged and give up. Instead, take a page from the lagom mentality and set a more realistic goal. Pick and exercise or class that you actually like going to. Even if all you can manage to start is yoga three times per week, that's much better than never going. If you're successful for a while, you may find you can add a bit more to your routine and gradually build up to a more robust fitness regimen over time. Or not, maybe 3 times per week is enough. Ultimately, just try to remember to have some balance.

If the thought of drinking glogg, eating decadent food and spending a lot of time relaxing gave you a bit of a stomach ache for its decadence, but you still liked some of the bigger concepts relating to hygge, this would be a good one to research further. It's also a good practice for when you've been able to have a lot of hygge time and need some balance.

The Lagom environmentalist

Lagom differs from hygge in that it focuses on an overall balance of everyday life. This reaches to considering how your day to day life impacts the planet. To incorporate lagom into your everyday life, remember to use as much water, waste and food as you need, but no more. Recycle. Don't produce unnecessary waste, and use water conservatively. Use more environmentally friendly energy options (think LED lights and solar power). As the population grows, our resources are becoming more scarce, so this is an important thing to keep in mind for living a balanced life.

You can make living a lagom lifestyle fun as well. If possible, you can grow some of your own vegetables, fruit and herbs in an effort to help lessen your environmental footprint. You can make gardening fun by planning out a pretty layout for your garden, enjoying the activity with a loved one, or joining gardening clubs in your community to make new friends. Just because an activity is about living sustainably, doesn't mean it can't also bring you joy. Another fun thing you can do is keep things like old cartons or toilet paper rolls for craft projects. Do them yourself or with your kids, or connect with a local teacher online to see if they are looking for craft resources.

Look into sustainability. This is especially important for when you are making choices about purchasing things like clothes and food. Buy locally when you can, and research where things come from – are the people making it earning a fair wage? Are the company's business practices environmentally friendly? When we look at food, there are a lot of things to consider – plant-based alternatives to meat and dairy significantly reduce your environmental footprint, but even beyond that, look deeper. Over using crops like corn and soy is also bad for the environment, so research a variety of vegetables and grains you can incorporate into your diet. Not only will this throw some fun variety into your food, but it will also be better for the environment in the long run.

Minimalism: how to build a lifestyle and mindset that gives you a level of mindfulness that will help you embrace hygge

The concept of minimalism offers from hygge significantly in some ways. While Hygge focuses on indulgence, minimalism is more akin to lagom in that it is also a philosophy that focuses on living with what you need.

The concepts, however, aren't totally exclusive of one another if we dig a little bit deeper. There are many different interpretations of how to live a minimalist lifestyle, and different versions of it out there as well. Ultimately, however, it's about rejecting the concept of mass consumerism that we have all been exposed to, particularly in the western world. Advertising demands that we constantly buy more, keep up with trends and make sure we always have the newest, shiniest thing. It also calls us to measure our value and our happiness but our productivity (how much money we can make) and encourages us to display that monetary value with status symbols. Expensive phones, flashy cars. When we reject the notion that material possessions should not be our priority, we are open to instead to focusing on other things in our lives that have true value. Our relationships and the contribution we make to our communities, and making them a better place for everyone.

This relates to hygge's emphasis on spending time with loved ones. Whereas minimalism encourages us to remember that our relationships with our friends and family should be our top priority, hygge accepts this as truth and embedded in its philosophy is the idea that spending some quality time with family and friends will help our sense of happiness.

Ultimately, minimalism is a bit more similar to lagom in that it's about seeking balance. Minimalism encourages us to strip away excess so we can focus our energy on what's important. The includes material items, but also how we spend our time and who we spend it with. It's liberating and sad all at once because it forces us to confront the reality that we do, in fact, only have a finite amount of time and resources, when we prefer to believe these things are infinite. We like to think there will always be a next time or a some day, but that isn't always true. Minimalism allows us to embrace this reality and, rather than cower, feel empowered by it. It lets us motivate ourselves with that notion that we must do what we want to do now, and not waste so much time on the frivolous or the unimportant. It's a tough reality to face at first, but it's one we all know and are simply denying. Once we face it, we can acknowledge it and confront it, which is ultimately a lot more liberating than denial.

CONCLUSION

At the end of the day, practicing a bit of hygge ultimately boils down to being consciously cozy. It boils down to spending time with people you love, and focusing on them individually while you do so, rather than in a large gathering. It means letting yourself indulge a little in life's more decadent things – rich food, hot beverages, a bit of sugar, and a bit of alcohol. It's letting yourself indulge in being a little lazy, and in spending time on a hobby that's more about creating and enjoying yourself than being productive. It's about making a point of creating warmth and light in the world when it gets the most dark and lighting a few candles. This may be in the dead of winter, but can also be found in other moments as well. When you're feeling down, homesick, lonely, melancholy on a rainy day, seeking out the joy in that setting, in that moment, letting yourself feel better and passing that resilience onto others so it can get even stronger is what hygge is all about.

So go, pick up a candle or a pair of fuzzy socks, just remember that's not really what it's about. It's about resilience, and most importantly, love.

Thank you for taking the time to read *More Than Just Candles*. If you enjoyed it, please consider telling your friends or posting a short review. Word of mouth is an author's best friend. Much appreciated.

Thank you,

EMMA JANSON.

Emma Janson

Made in the USA
Columbia, SC
23 January 2023

10862797R00065